GRAPEVINE BOOKS

THE LIFE AND MARTYRDOM OF POLYCARP

A COMPLETE ACCOUNT OF THE EARLY CHURCH BISHOP AND HIS LEGACY

Published by
GRAPEVINE BOOKS

www.grapevinebooks.com
email: contact@grapevinebooks.com

Ordering Information:
Quantity sales: Special discounts are available on quantity purchases by corporations, associations, and others.
For details, reach out to the publisher.

First published by Grapevine Books, 2025

CONTENTS

Epistle of Polycarp to the Philippians & Martyrdom of Polycarp: Apostolic Teaching and Testimony of an Early Church Father

(Bilingual English-Greek Edition)

INTRODUCTORY NOTE

TO THE EPISTLE OF POLYCARP TO THE PHILIPPIANS

The authenticity of the following Epistle can on no fair grounds be questioned. It is abundantly established by external testimony, and is also supported by the internal evidence. Irenæus says (*Adv. Hæreses*, iii. 3): ΕΣΤΙ δὲ καὶ Ἐπιστολὴ Πολυκάρπου πρὸς Φιλιππησίους γεγραμμένη, ἱκανωτάτη ἐξ ἧς καὶ τὸν χαρακτῆρα τῆς πίστεως αὐτοῦ, καὶ τὸ κήρυγμα τῆς ἀληθείας, οἱ βουλόμενοι, καὶ φροντίζοντες τῆς ἑαυτῶν σωτηρίας, δύνανται μαθεῖν. - "There is extant an Epistle of Polycarp written to the Philippians, most satisfactory, from which those that have a mind to do so may learn the character of his faith," etc. This passage is embodied by Eusebius in his *Ecclesiastical History* (iv. 14); and in another place the same writer refers to the Epistle before us as an undoubted production of Polycarp (*Hist. Eccl.*, iii. 36). Other ancient testimonies might easily be added, but are superfluous, inasmuch as there is a general consent among scholars at the present day that we have in this letter an authentic production of the renowned Bishop of Smyrna.

Of Polycarp's life little is known, but that little is highly interesting. Irenæus was his disciple, and tells us that "Polycarp was instructed by the apostles, and was brought into contact with many who had seen Christ." (*Adv. Hær.*, iii. 3) This passage was preserved by Eusebius, *Hist. Eccl.*, iv. 14, and he adds: Ὅ γέ τοι Πολύκαρπος ἐν τῇ δηλωθείσῃ πρὸς Φιλιππησίους αὐτοῦ γραφῇ, φερουμένῃ εἰς δεῦρο, κέχρηταί τισι μαρτυρίαις ἀπὸ τῆς Πέτρου προτέρας Ἐπιστολῆς. There is also a very graphic account given of Polycarp by Irenæus in his Epistle to Florinus, to which the reader is referred. It has been preserved by Eusebius (*Hist. Eccl.*, v. 20) and ends with: Καὶ ἐκ τῶν Ἐπιστολῶν δὲ αὐτοῦ ὧν ἐπέστειλεν, ἤτοι ταῖς γειτνιώσαις ἐκκλησίαις, ἐπιστηρίζων αὐτὰς, ἢ τῶν ἀδελφῶν τισὶ, νουθετῶν αὐτοὺς καὶ προτρεπόμενος, δύναται φανερωθῆναι. - «And this can be shown plainly from the letters which he sent, either to the neighboring churches for their confirmation, or to some of the brethren, admonishing and exhorting them."

The Epistle before us is not perfect in any of the Greek mss. which contain it. But the chapters wanting in Greek are contained in an ancient Latin version. While there is no ground for supposing, as some have done, that the whole Epistle is spurious, there seems considerable force in the arguments by which many others have sought to prove chap. xiii. to be an interpolation.

The date of the Epistle cannot be satisfactorily determined. It depends on the conclusion we reach as to some points, very difficult and obscure,

Polycarp to the Philippians

connected with that account of the martyrdom of Polycarp which has come down to us. We shall not, however, probably be far wrong if we fix it about the middle of the second century.

ΤΟΥ ΑΓΙΟΥ ΠΟΛΥΚΑΡΠΟΥ

ΕΠΙΣΚΟΠΟΥ ΣΜΥΡΝΗΣ ΚΑΙ ΙΕΡΟΜΑΡΤΥΡΟΣ

ΠΡΟΣ ΦΙΛΙΠΠΗΣΙΟΥΣ ΕΠΙΣΤΟΛΗ

From the Holy Polycarp,

Overseer of Smyrna, and Holy Martyr,

An Epistle to the Philippians

Introduction

Πολύκαρπος καὶ οἱ σὺν αὐτῳ πρεσβύτεροι τῇ ἐκκλησίᾳ τοῦ θεοῦ τῇ παροικούσῃ Φιλίππους· ἔλεος ὑμῖν καὶ εἰρήνη παρὰ θεοῦ παντοκράτορος καὶ Ἰησοῦ Χριστοῦ τοῦ σωτῆρος ἡμῶν πληθυνθείη.

Polycarp, and the elders with him, to the Church of God sojourning at Philippi: Mercy to you, and peace from God Almighty, and from the Lord Jesus Christ, our Savior, be multiplied.

Chapter 1

Praise of the Philippians

1:1 Συνεχάρην ὑμῖν μεγάλως ἐν τῷ κυρίῳ ἡμῶν Ἰησοῦ Χριστῷ, δεξαμένοις τὰ μιμήματα τῆς ἀληθοῦς ἀγάπης καὶ προπέμψασιν, ὡς ἐπέβαλεν ὑμῖν, τοὺς ἐνειλημένους τοῖς ἁγιοπρεπέσιν δεσμοῖς, ἅτινά ἐστιν διαδήματα τῶν ἀληθῶς ὑπὸ θεοῦ καὶ τοῦ κυρίου ἡμῶν ἐκλελεγμένων·

[1]I have greatly rejoiced with you in our Lord Jesus Christ, because ye have followed the example of true love [as displayed by God], and have accompanied, as became you, those who were bound in chains, the fitting ornaments of saints, and which are indeed the diadems of the true elect of God and our Lord;

1:2 καὶ ὅτι ἡ βεβαία τῆς πίστεως ὑμῶν ῥίζα, ἐξ ἀρχαίων καταγγελλομένη χρόνων, μέχρι νῦν διαμένει καὶ καρποφορεῖ εἰς τὸν κύριον ἡμῶν Ἰησοῦν Χριστόν, ὃς ὑπέμεινεν ὑπὲρ τῶν ἁμαρτιῶν ἡμῶν ἕως θανάτου κατανῆσαι, ὃν ἤγειρεν ὁ θεός, λύσας τὰς ὠδῖνας τοῦ ᾅδου·

[2]and because the strong root of your faith, spoken of in days long gone by, endures even until now, and brings forth fruit to our Lord Jesus Christ, who for our sins suffered even unto death, [but] “whom God raised from the dead, having loosed the bands of the grave.”

1:3 εἰς ὃν οὐκ ἰδόντες πιστεύετε χαρᾷ ἀνεκλαλήτῳ δεδοξασμένῃ, εἰς ἣν πολλοὶ ἐπιθυμοῦσιν εἰσελθεῖν, εἰδότες, ὅτι χάριτί ἐστε σεσωσμένοι, οὐκ ἐξ ἔργων, ἀλλὰ θελήματι θεοῦ διὰ Ἰησοῦ Χριστοῦ.

[3]“In whom, though now ye see Him not, ye believe, and believing, rejoice with joy unspeakable and full of glory;” into which joy many desire

to enter, knowing that "by grace ye are saved, not of works," but by the will of God through Jesus Christ.

Chapter 2

An Exhortation to Virtue

2:1 Διὸ ἀναζωσάμενοι τὰς ὀσφύας ὑμῶν δουλεύσατε τῷ θεῷ ἐν φόβῳ καὶ ἀληθείᾳ ἀπολιπόντες τὴν κενὴν ματαιολογίαν καὶ τὴν τῶν πολλῶν πλάνην, πιστεύσαντες εἰς τὸν ἐγείραντα τὸν κύριον ἡμῶν Ἰησοῦν Χριστὸν ἐκ νεκρῶν καὶ δόντα αὐτῷ δόξαν καὶ θρόνον ἐκ δεξιῶν αὐτοῦ· ᾧ πᾶσα πνοὴ λατρεύει, ὃς ἔρχεται κριτῆς ζώντων καὶ νεκρῶν, οὗ τὸ αἷμα ἐκζητήσει ὁ θεὸς ἀπὸ τῶν ἀπειθούντων αὐτῷ.

[1]"Wherefore, girding up your loins," "serve the Lord in fear" and truth, as those who have forsaken the vain, empty talk and error of the multitude, and "believed in Him who raised up our Lord Jesus Christ from the dead, and gave Him glory," and a throne at His right hand. To Him all things" in heaven and on earth are subject. Him every spirit serves. He comes as the Judge of the living and the dead. His blood will God require of those who do not believe in Him.

2:2 ὁ δὲ ἐγείρας αὐτὸν ἐκ νεκρῶν καὶ ἡμᾶς ἐγερεῖ, ἐὰν ποιῶμεν αὐτοῦ καὶ πορευώμεθα ἐν ταῖς ἐντολαῖς αὐτοῦ καὶ ἀγαπῶμεν ἃ ἠγάπησεν, ἀπεχόμενοι πάσης ἀδικίας, πλεονεξίας, φιλαργυρίας, καταλαλιᾶς, ψευδομαρτυρίας· μὴ ἀποδιδόντες κακὸν ἀντὶ κακοῦ ἢ λοιδορίαν ἀντὶ λοιδορίας ἢ γρόνθου ἀντὶ γρόνθου ἢ κατάραν ἀντὶ κατάρας·

[2]But He who raised Him up from the dead will raise up us also, if we do His will, and walk in His commandments, and love what He loved, keeping ourselves from all unrighteousness, covetousness, love of money, evil speaking, false witness; "not rendering evil for evil, or railing for railing," or blow for blow, or cursing for cursing,

2:3 μνημονεύοντες δὲ ὧν εἶπεν ὁ κύριος διδάσκων· Μὴ κρίνετε, ἵνα μὴ κριθῆτε· ᾧ μέτρῳ μετρεῖτε, ἀντιμετρηθήσεται ὑμῖν· καὶ ὅτι μακάριοι οἱ πτωχοὶ καὶ οἱ διωκόμενοι ἕνεκεν δικαιοσύνης, ὅτι αὐτῶν ἐστὶν ἡ βασιλεία τοῦ θεοῦ.

3but being mindful of what the Lord said in His teaching: "Judge not, that ye be not judged; forgive, and it shall be forgiven unto you; be merciful, that ye may obtain mercy; with what measure ye measure out, it shall be measured to you again; and once more, "Blessed are the poor, and those that are persecuted for righteousness' sake, for theirs is the kingdom of God."

Chapter 3

Expressions of Personal Unworthiness

3:1 Ταῦτα, ἀδελφοί, οὐκ ἐμαυτῷ ἐπτρέψας γράφω ὑμῖν περὶ τῆς δικαιοσύνης, ἀλλ' ἐπεὶ ὑμεῖς προεπεκαλέσασθέ με.

[1]These things, brethren, I write to you concerning righteousness, not because I take anything upon myself, but because ye have invited me to do so.

3:2οὔτεγὰρἐγὼοὔτεἄλλοςὅμοιοςἐμοὶδύναταικατακολουθῆσαι τῇ σοφίᾳ τοῦ μακαρίου καὶ ἐνδόξου Παύλου, ὃς γενόμενος ἐν ὑμῖν κατὰ πρόσωπον τῶν τότε ἀνθρώπων ἐδίδαξεν ἀκριβῶς καὶ βεβαίως τὸν περὶ ἀληθείας λόγον, ὃς καὶ ἀπὼν ὑμῖν ἔγραψεν ἐπιστολάς, εἰς ἃς ἐὰν εγκύπτητε, δυνηθήσεσθε οἰκοδομεῖσθαι εἰς τὴν δοθεῖσαν ὑμῖν πίστιν·

[2]For neither I, nor any other such one, can come up to the wisdom of the blessed and glorified Paul. He, when among you, accurately and steadfastly taught the word of truth in the presence of those who were then alive. And when absent from you, he wrote you letters, which, if you carefully study, you will find to be the means of building you up in that faith

3:3 ἥτις ἐστὶν μήτηρ πάντων ἡμῶν, ἐπακολουθούσης τῆς ἐλπίδος, προαγούσης τῆς εἰς θεὸν καὶ Χριστὸν καὶ εἰς τὸν πλησίον. ἐὰν γάρ τις τούτων ἐντὸς ᾖ, πεπλήρωκεν ἐντολὴν δικαιοσύνης· ὁ γὰρ ἔχων ἀγάπην μακράν ἐστιν πάσης ἁμαρτίας.

[3]which has been given you, and which, being followed by hope, and preceeded by love towards God, and Christ, and our neighbor, "is the mother of us all." For if any one be inwardly possessed of these graces, he hath fulfilled the command of righteousness, since he that hath love is far from all sin.

Chapter 4

Various Exhortations

4:1 Ἀρχὴ δὲ πάντων χαλεπῶν φιλαργυρία. εἰδότες οὖν ὅτι οὐδὲν εἰσηνέγκαμεν εἰς τὸν κόσμον, ἀλλ᾽ οὐδὲ ἐξενεγκεῖν τι ἔχομεν, ὁπλισώμεθα τοῖς ὅπλοις τῆς δικαιοσύνης καὶ διδάξωμεν ἑαυτοὺς πρῶτον προεύεσθαι ἐν τῇ ἐντολῇ τοῦ κυριοῦ·

1 "But the love of money is the root of all evils." Knowing, therefore, that "as we brought nothing into the world, so we can carry nothing out," let us arm ourselves with the armor of righteousness; and let us teach, first of all, ourselves to walk in the commandments of the Lord.

4:2 ἔπειτα καὶ τὰς γυναῖκας ἡμῶν ἐν τῇ δοθείσῃ αὐταῖς πίστει καὶ ἀγάπῃ καὶ ἁγνείᾳ στεργούσας τοὺς ἑαυτῶν ἄνδρας ἐν πάσῃ ἀληθείᾳ καὶ ἀγαπώσας πάντας ἐξ ἴσου ἐν πάσῃ ἐγκρατείᾳ, καὶ τὰ τέκνα παιδεύειν τὴν παιδείαν τοῦ φόβου τοῦ θεοῦ·

2Next, [teach] your wives [to walk] in the faith given to them, and in love and purity tenderly loving their own husbands in all truth, and loving all [others] equally in all chastity; and to train up their children in the knowledge and fear of God.

3 τὰς χήρας σωφρονούσας περὶ τὴν τοῦ κυρίου πίστιν, ἐντυγχανούσας ἀδιαλείπτως περὶ πάντων, μακρὰν οὔσας πάσης διαβολῆς, καταλαλιᾶς, ψευδομαρτυρίας, φιλαργυρίας καὶ παντὸς κακοῦ, γινωσκούσας ὅτι εἰσὶ θυσιαστήριον θεοῦ καὶ ὅτι πάντα μωμοσκοπεῖται, καὶ λέληθεν αὐτὸν οὐδὲν οὔτε λογισμῶν οὔτε ἐννοιῶν οὔτε τι τῶν κρυπτῶν τῆς καρδίας.

3Teach the widows to be discreet as respects the faith of the Lord, praying continually for all, being far from all slandering, evil-speaking,

Polycarp to the Philippians

false-witnessing, love of money, and every kind of evil; knowing that they are the altars of God, that He clearly perceives all things, and that nothing is hidden from Him, neither reasonings, nor reflections, nor any one of the secret things of the heart.

Chapter 5

The Duties of Deacons, Youths, and Virgins

1. Εἰδότες, οὖν ὅτι θεὸς οὐ μυκτηρίζεται, ὀφείλομεν ἀξίως τῆς ἐντολῆς αὐτοῦ καὶ δόξης περιπατεῖν.

1.Knowing, then, that "God is not mocked," we ought to walk worthy of

His commandment and glory.

2.ὁμοίως διάκονοι ἄμεμπτοι κατενώπιον αὐτοῦ τῆς δικαιοσύνης ὡς θεοῦ καὶ Χριστοῦ διάκονοι καὶ οὐκ ἀνθρώπων· μὴ διαβολοι, μὴ δίλογοι ἀφιλάργυροι, ἐγκρατεῖς περὶ πάντα, εὔσπλαγχνοι, ἐπιμελεῖς, πορευόμενοι κατὰ τὴν ἀλήθειαν τοῦ κυρίου, ὃς ἐγένετο διάκονος πάντων· ᾧ ἐὰν εὐαρεστήσωμεν ἐν τῷ νῦν αἰῶνι, ἀποληψόμεθα καὶ τὸν μέλλοντα, καθὼς ὑπέσχετο ἡμῖν ἐγεῖραι ἡμᾶς ἐκ νεκρῶν, καὶ ὅτι ἐὰν πολιτευσώμεθα ἀξίως αὐτοῦ, καὶ συμβασιλεύσομεν αὐτῷ, ἔγε πιστεύομεν.

2.In like manner should the deacons be blameless before the face of His righteousness, as being the servants of God and Christ, and not of men. They must not be slanderers, two-faced, or lovers of money, but temperate in all things, compassionate, industrious, walking according to the truth of the Lord, who was the servant of all. If we please Him in this present world, we shall receive also the future world, according as He has promised to us that He will raise us again from the dead, and that if we live worthily of Him,

"we shall also reign together with Him," provided only we believe.

3. ὁμοίως καὶ νεώτεροι ἄμεμπτοι ἐν πᾶσιν, πρὸ παντὸς προνοοῦντες ἁγνείας καὶ χαλιναγωγοῦντες ἑαυτοὺς ἀπὸ τῶν ἐπιθυμιῶν ἐν τῷ κόσμῳ, ὅτι πᾶσα ἐπιθυμία κατὰ τοῦ πνεύματος

στρατεύεται, καὶ οὔτε πόρνοι οὔτε μαλακοὶ οὔτε ἀρσενοκοῖται βασιλείαν θεοῦ κληρονομήσουσιν, οὔτε οἱ ποιοῦντες τὰ ἄτοπα. διό δέον ἀπέχεσθαι ἀπὸ πάντων τούτων, ὑποτασσομένους τοῖς πρεσβυτέροις καὶ διακόνοις ὡς θεῷ καὶ Χριστῷ· τὰς παρθένους ἐν ἀμώμῳ καὶ ἁγνῇ συνειδήσει περιπατεῖν.

[3]In like manner, let the young men also be blameless in all things, being especially careful to preserve purity, and keeping themselves in, as with a bridle, from every kind of evil. For it is well that they should be cut off from the lusts that are in the world, since "every lust warreth against the spirit; " and "neither fornicators, nor effeminate, nor abusers of themselves with mankind, shall inherit the kingdom of God," nor those who do things inconsistent and unbecoming. Wherefore, it is needful to abstain from all these things, being subject to the presbyters and deacons, as unto God and Christ. The virgins also must walk in a blameless and pure conscience.

Chapter 6

The Duties of Elders and Others

6:1 Καὶ οἱ πρεσβύτεροι δὲ εὔσπλαγχνοι εἰς πάντας ἐλεήμονες, ἐπιστρέφοντες τὰ ἀποπεπλανημένα, ἐπισκεπτόμενοι πάνας ἀσθενεῖς, μὴ ἀμελοῦντες χήρας ἢ ὀρφανοῦ ἢ πένητος· ἀλλὰ προνοοῦτες ἀεὶ τοῦ καλοῦ ἐνώπιον θεοῦ καὶ ἀνθρώπων, ἀπεχόμενοι πάσης ὀργῆς, προσωποληψίας, μὴ ταχέως πιστεύοντες κατά τινος, μὴ ἀπότομοι ἐν κρίσει, εἰδότες ὅτι πάντες ὀφειλέται ἐσμὲν ἁμαρτίας.

And let the presbyters be compassionate and merciful to all, bringing back those that wander, visiting all the sick, and not neglecting the widow, the orphan, or the poor, but always "providing for that which is becoming in the sight of God and man; "abstaining from all wrath, respect of persons, and unjust judgment; keeping far off from. all covetousness, not quickly crediting [an evil report] against any one, not severe in judgment, as knowing that we are all under a debt of sin.

6:2. εἰ οὖν δεόμεθα τοῦ κυρίου, ἵνα ἡμῖν ἀφῇ, ὀφείλομεν καὶ ἡμεῖς ἀφιέναι· ἀπέναντι γὰρ τῶν τοῦ κυρίου καὶ θεοῦ ἐσμὲν ὀφθαλμῶν, καὶ πάντας δεῖ παραστῆναι τῷ βήματι τοῦ Χριστοῦ καὶ ἕκαστον ὑπέρ αὐτοῦ λόγον δοῦναι.

[2]If then we entreat the Lord to forgive us, we ought also ourselves to forgive; for we are before the eyes of our Lord and God, and "we must all appear at the judgment-seat of Christ, and everyone must give an account of himself."

6:3 οὕτως οὖν δουλεύσωμεν αὐτῷ μετὰ φόβου καὶ πάσης εὐλαβείας, καθὼς αὐτὸς ἐνετείλατο καὶ οἱ εὐαγγελισάμενοι ἡμᾶς ἀπόσολοι καὶ οἱ προφῆται, οἱ προκηρύξαντες τὴν ἔλευσιν τοῦ κυρίου ἡμῶν· ζηλωταὶ περὶ τὸ καλόν, ἀπεχόμενοι τῶν σκανδάλων καὶ τῶν ψευδαδέλφων καὶ τῶν ἐν ὑποκρίσει φερόντων τὸ ὄνομα τοῦ κυρίου, οἵτινες ἀποπλανῶσι κενοὺς ἀνθρώπους.

3 Let us then serve Him in fear, and with all reverence, even as He Himself has commanded us, and as the apostles who preached the Gospel unto us, and the prophets who proclaimed beforehand the coming of the Lord [have alike taught us]. Let us be zealous in the pursuit of that which is good, keeping ourselves from causes of offence, from false brethren, and from those who in hypocrisy bear the name of the Lord, and draw away vain men into error.

Chapter 7

Avoid the Docetae, and Persevere in Fasting and Prayer

7:1 Πᾶς γὰρ ὃς ἂν μὴ ὁμολογῇ Ἰησοῦν Χριστὸν ἐν σαρκὶ ἐληλυθέναι, ἀντιχριστός ἐστιν· καὶ ὃς ἂν μὴ ὁμολογῇ τὸ μαρτύριον τοῦ σταυροῦ, ἐκ τοῦ διαβόλου ἐστίν· καὶ ὃς ἂν μεθοδεύῃ τὰ λόγια τοῦ κυρίου πρὸς τὰς ἰδίας ἐπιθυμίας καὶ λέγῃ μήτε ἀνάστασιν μήτε κρίσιν, οὗτος πρωτότοκός ἐστι τοῦ σατανᾶ.

1."For whoever does not confess that Jesus Christ has come in the flesh, is antichrist;" and whoever does not confess the testimony of the cross, is of the devil; and whoever perverts the oracles of the Lord to his own lusts, and says that there is neither a resurrection nor a judgment, he is the first-born of Satan.

Polycarp to the Philippians

7:2 διὸ ἀπολιπόντες τὴν ματαιότητα τῶν πολλῶν καὶ τὰς ψευδοδιδασκαλίας ἐπὶ τὸν ἐξ ἀρχῆς ἡμῖν παραδοθέντα λόγον ἐπιστρέψωμεν, νήφοντες πρὸς τὰς εὐχὰς καὶ προσκαρτεροῦντες νηστείας, δεήσεσιν αἰτούμενοι τὸν παντεπόπτην θεὸν μὴ εἰσενεγκεῖν ἡμᾶς εἰς πειρασμόν, καθὼς εἶπεν ὁ κύριος· Τὸ μὲν πνεῦμα πρόθυμον, ἡ δὲ σὰρξ ἀσθενής.

2.Wherefore, forsaking the vanity of many, and their false doctrines, let us return to the word which has been handed down to us from the beginning;

"watching unto prayer," and persevering in fasting; beseeching in our supplications the all-seeing God to "not lead us into temptation." As the Lord has said: "The spirit truly is willing, but the flesh is weak."

Chapter 8

Persevere in Hope and Patience

8:1. Ἀδιαλείπτως οὖν προσκαρτερῶμεν τῇ ἐλπίδι ἡμῶν καὶ τῷ ἀρραβῶνι τῆς δικαιοσύνης ἡμῶν, ὅς ἐστι Χριστὸς Ἰησοῦς, ὃς ἀνήγκεν ἡμῶν τὰς ἁμαρτίας τῷ ἰδίῳ σώματι ἐπὶ τὸ ξύλον, ὃς ἁμαρτίαν οὐκ ἐποίησεν, οὐδὲ εὑρέθη δόλος ἐν τῷ στόματι αὐτοῦ· ἀλλὰ δι' ἡμᾶς, ἵνα ζήσωμεν ἐν αὐτῷ, πάντα ὑπέμεινεν.

1.Let us then continually persevere in our hope, and the earnest of our righteousness, which is Jesus Christ, "who bore our sins in His own body on the tree," "who did no sin, neither was guile found in His mouth," but endured all things for us, that we might live in Him.

8:2. μιμηταὶ οὖν γενώμεθα τῆς ὑπομονῆς αὐτοῦ, καὶ ἐὰν πάσχωμεν διὰ τὸ ὄνομα αὐτοῦ, δοξάζωμεν αὐτόν. τοῦτον γὰρ ἡμῖν τὸν ὑπογραμμὸν ἔθηκε δι' ἑαυτοῦ, καὶ ἡμεῖς τοῦτο ἐπιστεύσαμεν.

2.Let us then be imitators of His patience; and if we suffer for His name's sake, let us glorify Him. For He has set us this example in Himself, and we have believed that such is the case.

Chapter 9

Patience Inculcated

9:1. Παρακαλῶ οὖν πάντας ὑμᾶς, πειθαρχεῖν τῷ λόγῳ τῆς δικαιοσύνης καὶ ἀσκεῖν πᾶσαν ὑπομονήν, ἣν καὶ εἴδατε κατ' ὀφθαλμοὺς οὐ μόνον ἐν τοῖς μακαρίοις Ἰγνατίῳ καὶ Ζωσίμῳ καὶ Ῥούφῳ, ἀλλὰ καὶ ἐν ἄλλοις τοῖς ἐξ ὑμῶν καὶ ἐν αὐτῷ Παύλῳ καὶ τοῖς λοιποις ἀποστόλοις·

1.I exhort you all, therefore, to yield obedience to the word of righteousness, and to exercise all patience, such as ye have seen [set] before your eyes, not only in the case of the blessed Ignatius, and Zosimus, and Rufus, but also in others among yourselves, and in Paul himself, and the rest of the apostles.

9:2. πεπεισμένους ὅτι οὗτοι πάντες οὐκ εἰς κενὸν ἔδραμον, ἀλλ' ἐν πίστει καὶ δικαιοσύνῃ, καὶ ὅτι εἰς τὸν ὀφειλόμενον αὐτοῖς τόπον εἰσὶ παρὰ τῷ κυρίῳ, ᾧ καὶ συνέπαθον. οὐ γὰρ τὸν νῦν ἠγάπησαν αἰῶνα, ἀλλὰ τὸν ὑπέρ ἡμῶν ἀποθανόντα καὶ δι' ἡμᾶς ὑπὸ τοῦ θεοῦ ἀναστάντα.

2.[This do] in the assurance that all these have not run in vain, but in faith and righteousness, and that they are [now] in their due place in the presence of the Lord, with whom also they suffered. For they loved not this present world, but Him who died for us, and for our sakes was raised again by God from the dead.

Chapter 10

Exhortation to the Practice of Virtue

10:1 In his ergo state et domini exemplar sequimini, firmi in fide et immutabiles, fraternitatis amatores, diligentes invicem, in veritate sociati, mansuetudine domini alterutri praestolantes, nullum despicientes.

1.Stand fast, therefore, in these things, and follow the example of the Lord, being firm and unchangeable in the faith, loving the brotherhood, and being attached to one another, joined together in the truth, exhibiting the meekness of the Lord in your interaction with one another, and despising no one.

10:2 Cum possitis benefacere, nolite differre, quia eleëmosyna de morte liberat. Omnes vobis invicem subiecti estote, conversationem vestram irreprensibilem habentes in gentibus, ut ex bonis operibus vestris et vos laudem accipiatis et dominus in vobis non blasphemetur.

2.When you can do good, defer it not, because "alms delivers from death." Be all of you subject one to another, having your conduct blameless among the Gentiles, that ye may both receive praise for your good works, and the Lord may not be blasphemed through you.

10:3. Vae autem per quem nomen domini blasphematur. Sobrietatem ergo docete omnes in qua et vos conversamini.

3.But woe to him by whom the name of the Lord is blasphemed! Teach, therefore, sobriety to all, and manifest it also in your own conduct.

Chapter 11

Exhortation of Grief on Account of Valens

11:1 Nimis contristatus sum pro Valente, qui presbyter factus est aliquando apud vos, quod sic ignoret is locum qui datus est ei. Moneo itaque ut abstinete vos ab omni malo.

1.I am greatly grieved for Valens, who was once a presbyter among you, because he so little understands the place that was given him [in the Church]. I exhort you, therefore, that ye abstain from covetousness, and that ye be chaste and truthful. “Abstain from every form of evil.”

11:2 Qui autem non potest se in his gubernare, quomodo alii pronuntiat hoc? Si quis non se abstinuerit ab avaritia, ab idolotatria conquinabitur et

Polycarp to the Philippians

tamquam inter gentes iudicabitur, qui ignorant iudicium domini. Aut nescimus, quia sancti mundum iudicabunt? sicut Paulus docet.

2.For if a man cannot govern himself in such matters, how shall he enjoin them on others? If a man does not keep himself from covetousness, he shall be defiled by idolatry, and shall be judged as one of the heathen.

But who of us are ignorant of the judgment of the Lord? “Do we not know that the saints shall judge the world?” as Paul teaches.

11:3 Ego autem nihil tale sensi in vobis vel audivi, in quibus laboravit beatus Paulus, qui estis in principio episulae eius. De vobis etenim gloriatur in omnibus ecclesiis, quae dominum solae tunc cognoverant; nos autem nondum cognoveramus.

3.But I have neither seen nor heard of any such thing among you, in the midst of whom the blessed Paul labored, and who are commended in the beginning of his Epistle. For he boasts of you in all those Churches which alone then knew the Lord; but we [of Smyrna] had not yet known Him.

11:4 Valde ergo, fratres, constristor pro illo et pro coniuge eius, quibus det dominus paenitentiam veram. Sobrii ergo estote et vos in hoc; et non sicut inimicos tales existimetis, sed sicut passibilia membra et errantia eos revocate, ut omnium vestrum corpus salvetis. Hoc enim agentes vos ipsos aedificatis.

I am deeply grieved, therefore, brethren, for him (Valens) and his wife; to whom may the Lord grant true repentance! 4 And be ye then moderate in regard to this matter, and "do not count such as enemies," but call them back as suffering and straying members, that ye may save your whole body. For by so acting ye shall edify yourselves.

Chapter 12

12:1 Confido enim vos bene exercitatos esse in sacris literis et nihil vos latet; mihi autem non est concessum. Modo, ut his scripturis dictum est, irascimini et nolite peccare, et sol non occidat super iracundiam vestram. Beatus, qui meminerit; quod ego credo esse in vobis.

1.For I trust that ye are well versed in the Sacred Scriptures, and that nothing is hidden from you; but to me this privilege is not yet granted. It is declared then in these Scriptures, "Be ye angry, and sin not," and, "Let not the sun go down upon your wrath." Happy is he who remembers this, which I believe to be the case with you.

12:2 Deus autem et pater domini nostri Iesu Christi, et ipse sempiternus pontifex, dei filius Iesus Christus, aedificet vos in fide et veritate et in omni mansuetudine et sine iracundia et in patientia et in longanimitate et tolerantia et castitate; et det vobis sortem et partem inter sanctos suos et nobis vobiscum et omnibus, qui sunt sub caelo, qui credituri sunt in dominum nostrum et deum Iesum Christum et in ipsius patrem, qui resuscitavit eum a mortuis.

2.But may the God and Father of our Lord Jesus Christ, and Jesus Christ Himself, who is the Son of God, and our everlasting High Priest, build you up in faith and truth, and in all meekness, gentleness, patience, long-suffering, forbearance, and purity; and may He bestow on you a lot and portion among His saints, and on us with you, and on all who are under heaven, who shall believe in our Lord Jesus Christ, and in His Father, who "raised Him from the dead.

12:3 Pro omnibus sanctis orate. Orate etiam pro regibus et potestatibus et principibus atque pro persequentibus et odientibus vos et pro inimicis crucis, ut fructus vester manifestus sit in omnibus, ut sitis in illo perfecti.

3.Pray for all the saints. Pray also for kings, and potentates, and princes, and for those that persecute and hate you, and for the enemies of the cross, that your fruit may be manifest to all, and that ye may be perfect in Him.

Chapter 13

13:1 Ἐγράψατέ μοι καὶ ὑμεῖς καὶ Ἰγνάτιος, ἵν', ἐάν τις ἀπέρχηται εἰς Σρίαν, καὶ τὰ παρ' ὑμῶν ἀποκομίσῃ γράμματα· ὅπερ ποιήσω, ἐὰν λάβω καιρὸν εὔθετον, εἴτε ἐγώ, εἴτε ὃν πέμπω πρεσβεύσοντα καὶ περὶ ὑμῶν.

Both you and Ignatius wrote to me, that if any one went [from this] into Syria, he should carry your letter with him; which request I will attend to if I find a fitting opportunity, either personally, or through some other acting for me, that your desire may be fulfilled.

13:2 τὰς ἐπιστολὰς Ἰγνατίου τὰς περμφθείσας ἡμῖν ὑπ' αὐτοῦ καὶ ἄλλας, ὅσας εἴχομεν παρ' ἡμῖν, ἐπέμψαμεν ὑμῖν, καθὼς ἐνετείλασθε· αἵτινες ὑποτεταγμέναι εἰσὶν τῇ ἐπιστολῇ ταύτῃ, ἐξ ὧν μεγάλα ὠφεληθῆναι δυνήσεσθε. περιέχουσιν γὰρ πίστιν καὶ ὑπομονὴν καὶ πᾶσαν οἰκοδομὴν τὴν εἰς τὸν κύριον ἡμῶν ἀνήκουσαν. *Et de ipso Ignatio et de his, qui cum eo sunt, quod certius agnoveritis significate.*

2.The Epistles of Ignatius written by him to us, and all the rest [of his Epistles] which we have by us, we have sent to you, as you requested. They are subjoined to this Epistle, and by them ye may be greatly profited; for they treat of faith and patience, and all things that tend to edification in our Lord. Any more certain information you may have obtained respecting both Ignatius himself, and those that were with him, have the goodness to make known to us.

Chapter 14

14:1 Haec vobis scripsi per Crescentem, quem in praesenti commendavi vobis et nunc commendo. Conversatus est enim nobiscum inculpabiliter; credo quia et vobiscum similiter. Sororem autem eius habebitis commendatam, eum venerit ad vos. Incolumes estote in domino Iesu Christo in gratia eum omnibus vestris. Amen.

These things I have written to you by Crescens, whom up to the present time I have recommended unto you, and do now recommend. For he has acted blamelessly among us, and I believe also among you. Moreover, ye

will hold his sister in esteem when she comes to you. Be ye safe in the Lord Jesus Christ. Grace be with you all. Amen.

The Greek and Latin Text Alone:

ΤΟΥ ΑΓΙΟΥ ΠΟΛΥΚΑΡΠΟΥ

ΕΠΙΣΚΟΠΟΥ ΣΜΥΡΝΗΣ ΚΑΙ ΙΕΡΟΜΑΡΤΥΡΟΣ

ΠΡΟΣ ΦΙΛΙΠΠΗΣΙΟΥΣ ΕΠΙΣΤΟΛΗ

Πολύκαρπος καὶ οἱ σὺν αὐτῳ πρεσβύτεροι τῇ ἐκκλησίᾳ τοῦ θεοῦ τῇ παροικούσῃ Φιλίππους· ἔλεος ὑμῖν καὶ εἰρήνη παρὰ θεοῦ παντοκράτορος καὶ Ἰησοῦ Χριστοῦ τοῦ σωτῆρος ἡμῶν πληθυνθείη.

I

1.Συνεχάρην ὑμῖν μεγάλως ἐν τῷ κυρίῳ ἡμῶν Ἰησοῦ Χριστῷ,

δεξαμένοις τὰ μιμήματα τῆς ἀληθοῦς ἀγάπης καὶ προπέμψασιν, ὡς ἐπέβαλεν ὑμῖν, τοὺς ἐνειλημένους τοῖς ἁγιοπρεπέσιν δεσμοῖς, ἅτινά ἐστιν διαδήματα τῶν ἀληθῶς ὑπὸ θεοῦ καὶ τοῦ κυρίου ἡμῶν ἐκλελεγμένων· 2. καὶ ὅτι ἡ βεβαία τῆς πίστεως ὑμῶν ῥίζα, ἐξ ἀρχαίων καταγγελλομένη χρόνων, μέχρι νῦν διαμένει καὶ καρποφορεῖ εἰς τὸν κύριον ἡμῶν Ἰησοῦν Χριστόν, ὃς ὑπέμεινεν ὑπὲρ τῶν ἁμαρτιῶν ἡμῶν ἕως θανάτου καταντῆσαι, ὃν ἤγειρεν ὁ θεός, λύσας τὰς ὠδῖνας τοῦ ᾅδου· 3. εἰς ὃν οὐκ ἰδόντες πιστεύετε χαρᾷ ἀνεκλαλήτῳ δεδοξασμένῃ, εἰς ἣν πολλοὶ ἐπιθυμοῦσιν εἰσελθεῖν, εἰδότες, ὅτι χάριτί ἐστε σεσωσμένοι, οὐκ ἐξ ἔργων, ἀλλὰ θελήματι θεοῦ διὰ Ἰησοῦ Χριστοῦ.

II

1.Διὸ ἀναζωσάμενοι τὰς ὀσφύας ὑμῶν δουλεύσατε τῷ θεῷ ἐν φόβῳ καὶ ἀληθείᾳ ἀπολιπόντες τὴν κενὴν ματαιολογίαν καὶ τὴν τῶν πολλῶν πλάνην, πιστεύσαντες εἰς τὸν ἐγείραντα τὸν κύριον ἡμῶν Ἰησοῦν Χριστὸν ἐκ νεκρῶν καὶ δόντα αὐτῷ δόξαν καὶ θρόνον ἐκ δεξιῶν αὐτοῦ· ᾧ πᾶσα πνοὴ λατρεύει, ὃς ἔρχεται κριτῆς ζώντων καὶ νεκρῶν, οὗ τὸ αἷμα ἐκζητήσει ὁ θεὸς ἀπὸ τῶν ἀπειθούντων αὐτῷ. 2. ὁ δὲ ἐγείρας αὐτὸν ἐκ νεκρῶν καὶ ἡμᾶς ἐγερεῖ, ἐὰν ποιῶμεν αὐτοῦ καὶ πορευώμεθα ἐν ταῖς ἐντολαῖς αὐτοῦ καὶ ἀγαπῶμεν ἃ ἠγάπησεν, ἀπεχόμενοι πάσης ἀδικίας, πλεονεξίας, φιλαργυρίας, καταλαλιᾶς, ψευδομαρτυρίας· μὴ ἀποδιδόντες κακὸν ἀντὶ κακοῦ ἢ λοιδορίαν ἀντὶ λοιδορίας ἢ γρόνθου ἀντὶ γρόνθου ἢ κατάραν ἀντὶ κατάρας· 3. μνημονεύοντες δὲ ὧν εἶπεν ὁ κύριος διδάσκων· Μὴ κρίνετε, ἵνα μὴ κριθῆτε· ᾧ μέτρῳ μετρεῖτε, ἀντιμετρηθήσεται ὑμῖν· καὶ ὅτι μακάριοι οἱ πτωχοὶ καὶ οἱ διωκόμενοι ἕνεκεν δικαιοσύνης, ὅτι αὐτῶν ἐστὶν ἡ βασιλεία τοῦ θεοῦ.

III

1.Ταῦτα, ἀδελφοί, οὐκ ἐμαυτῷ ἐπτρέψας γράφω ὑμῖν περὶ τῆς δικαιοσύνης, ἀλλ᾽ ἐπεὶ ὑμεῖς προεπεκαλέσασθέ με. 2. οὔτε γὰρ ἐγὼ οὔτε ἄλλος ὅμοιος ἐμοὶ δύναται κατακολουθῆσαι τῇ σοφίᾳ τοῦ μακαρίου καὶ ἐνδόξου Παύλου, ὃς γενόμενος ἐν ὑμῖν κατὰ πρόσωπον τῶν τότε ἀνθρώπων ἐδίδαξεν ἀκριβῶς καὶ βεβαίως τὸν περὶ ἀληθείας λόγον, ὃς καὶ ἀπὼν ὑμῖν ἔγραψεν ἐπιστολάς, εἰς ἃς ἐὰν εγκύπτητε, δυνηθήσεσθε οἰκοδομεῖσθαι εἰς τὴν

δοθεῖσαν ὑμῖν πίστιν· 3. ἥτις ἐστὶν μήτηρ πάντων ἡμῶν, ἐπακολουθούσης τῆς ἐλπίδος, προαγούσης τῆς εἰς θεὸν καὶ Χριστὸν καὶ εἰς τὸν πλησίον. ἐὰν γάρ τις τούτων ἐντὸς ᾖ, πεπλήρωκεν ἐντολὴν δικαιοσύνης· ὁ γὰρ ἔχων ἀγάπην μακράν ἐστιν πάσης ἁμαρτίας.

IV

1.Ἀρχὴ δὲ πάντων χαλεπῶν φιλαργυρία. εἰδότες οὖν ὅτι οὐδὲν εἰσηνέγκαμεν εἰς τὸν κόσμον, ἀλλ' οὐδὲ ἐξενεγκεῖν τι ἔχομεν, ὁπλισώμεθα τοῖς ὅπλοις τῆς δικαιοσύνης καὶ διδάξωμεν ἑαυτοὺς πρῶτον προεύεσθαι ἐν τῇ ἐντολῇ τοῦ κυριοῦ· 2. ἔπειτα καὶ τὰς γυναῖκας ἡμῶν ἐν τῇ δοθείσῃ αὐταῖς πίστει καὶ ἀγάπῃ καὶ ἁγνείᾳ στεργούσας τοὺς ἑαυτῶν ἄνδρας ἐν πάσῃ ἀληθείᾳ καὶ ἀγαπώσας πάντας ἐξ ἴσου ἐν πάσῃ ἐγκρατείᾳ, καὶ τὰ τέκνα παιδεύειν τὴν παιδείαν τοῦ φόβου τοῦ θεοῦ· 3. τὰς χήρας σωφρονούσας περὶ τὴν τοῦ κυρίου πίστιν, ἐντυγχανούσας ἀδιαλείπτως περὶ πάντων, μακρὰν οὔσας πάσης διαβολῆς, καταλαλιᾶς, ψευδομαρτυρίας, φιλαργυρίας καὶ παντὸς κακοῦ, γινωσκούσας ὅτι εἰσὶ θυσιαστήριον θεοῦ καὶ ὅτι πάντα μωμοσκοπεῖται, καὶ λέληθεν αὐτὸν οὐδὲν οὔτε λογισμῶν οὔτε ἐννοιῶν οὔτε τι τῶν κρυπτῶν τῆς καρδίας.

V

1.Εἰδότες, οὖν ὅτι θεὸς οὐ μυκτηρίζεται, ὀφείλομεν ἀξίως τῆς ἐντολῆς αὐτοῦ καὶ δόξης περιπατεῖν. 2. ὁμοίως διάκονοι ἄμεμπτοι κατενώπιον αὐτοῦ τῆς δικαιοσύνης ὡς θεοῦ καὶ Χριστοῦ διάκονοι καὶ οὐκ ἀνθρώπων· μὴ διαβολοι, μὴ δίλογοι ἀφιλάργυροι, ἐγκρατεῖς περὶ πάντα, εὔσπλαγχνοι, ἐπιμελεῖς, πορευόμενοι κατὰ τὴν ἀλήθειαν τοῦ κυρίου, ὃς ἐγένετο διάκονος πάντων· ᾧ ἐὰν εὐαρεστήσωμεν ἐν τῷ νῦν αἰῶνι, ἀποληψόμεθα καὶ τὸν μέλλοντα, καθὼς ὑπέσχετο ἡμῖν ἐγεῖραι ἡμᾶς ἐκ νεκρῶν, καὶ ὅτι ἐὰν πολιτευσώμεθα ἀξίως αὐτοῦ, καὶ συμβασιλεύσομεν αὐτῷ, ἔγε πιστεύομεν. 3. ὁμοίως καὶ νεώτεροι ἄμεμπτοι ἐν πᾶσιν, πρὸ παντὸς προνοοῦντες ἁγνείας καὶ χαλιναγωγοῦντες ἑαυτοὺς ἀπὸ τῶν ἐπιθυμιῶν ἐν τῷ κόσμῳ, ὅτι πᾶσα ἐπιθυμία κατὰ τοῦ πνεύματος στρατεύεται, καὶ οὔτε πόρνοι οὔτε μαλακοὶ οὔτε ἀρσενοκοῖται βασιλείαν θεοῦ κληρονομήσουσιν, οὔτε οἱ ποιοῦντες τὰ ἄτοπα. διό δέον ἀπέχεσθαι ἀπὸ πάντων τούτων, ὑποτασσομένους τοῖς πρεσβυτέροις καὶ διακόνοις ὡς θεῷ καὶ Χριστῷ· τὰς παρθένους ἐν ἀμώμῳ καὶ ἁγνῇ συνειδήσει περιπατεῖν.

VI

1.Καὶ οἱ πρεσβύτεροι δὲ εὔσπλαγχνοι εἰς πάντας ἐλεήμονες, ἐπιστρέφοντες τὰ ἀποπεπλανημένα, ἐπισκεπτόμενοι πάνας ἀσθενεῖς, μὴ ἀμελοῦντες χήρας ἢ ὀρφανοῦ ἢ πένητος· ἀλλὰ προνοοῦτες ἀεὶ τοῦ καλοῦ ἐνώπιον θεοῦ καὶ ἀνθρώπων, ἀπεχόμενοι πάσης ὀργῆς, προσωποληψίας, μὴ ταχέως πιστεύοντες κατά τινος, μὴ ἀπότομοι ἐν κρίσει, εἰδότες ὅτι πάντες ὀφειλέται ἐσμὲν ἁμαρτίας. 2. εἰ οὖν δεόμεθα τοῦ κυρίου, ἵνα ἡμῖν ἀφῇ, ὀφείλομεν καὶ ἡμεῖς ἀφιέναι· ἀπέναντι γὰρ τῶν τοῦ κυρίου καὶ θεοῦ ἐσμὲν ὀφθαλμῶν, καὶ πάντας δεῖ παραστῆναι τῷ βήματι τοῦ Χριστοῦ καὶ ἕκαστον ὑπέρ αὐτοῦ λόγον δοῦναι. 3. οὕτως οὖν δουλεύσωμεν αὐτῷ μετὰ φόβου καὶ πάσης εὐλαβείας, καθὼς αὐτὸς ἐνετείλατο καὶ οἱ εὐαγγελισάμενοι ἡμᾶς

ἀπόσολοι καὶ οἱ προφῆται, οἱ προκηρύξαντες τὴν ἔλευσιν τοῦ κυρίου ἡμῶν· ζηλωταὶ περὶ τὸ καλόν, ἀπεχόμενοι τῶν σκανδάλων καὶ τῶν ψευδαδέλφων καὶ τῶν ἐν ὑποκρίσει φερόντων τὸ ὄνομα τοῦ κυρίου, οἵτινες ἀποπλανῶσι κενοὺς ἀνθρώπους.

VII

1.Πᾶς γὰρ ὃς ἂν μὴ ὁμολογῇ Ἰησοῦν Χριστὸν ἐν σαρκὶ ἐληλυθέναι, ἀντιχριστός ἐστιν· καὶ ὃς ἂν μὴ ὁμολογῇ τὸ μαρτύριον τοῦ σταυροῦ, ἐκ τοῦ διαβόλου ἐστίν· καὶ ὃς ἂν μεθοδεύῃ τὰ λόγια τοῦ κυρίου πρὸς τὰς ἰδίας ἐπιθυμίας καὶ λέγῃ μήτε ἀνάστασιν μήτε κρίσιν, οὗτος πρωτότοκός ἐστι τοῦ σατανᾶ. 2. διὸ ἀπολιπόντες τὴν ματαιότητα τῶν πολλῶν καὶ τὰς ψευδοδιδασκαλίας ἐπὶ τὸν ἐξ ἀρχῆς ἡμῖν παραδοθέντα λόγον ἐπιστρέψωμεν, νήφοντες πρὸς τὰς εὐχὰς καὶ προσκαρτεροῦντες νηστείας, δεήσεσιν αἰτούμενοι τὸν παντεπόπτην θεὸν μὴ εἰσενεγκεῖν ἡμᾶς εἰς πειρασμόν, καθὼς εἶπεν ὁ κύριος· Τὸ μὲν πνεῦμα πρόθυμον, ἡ δὲ σὰρξ ἀσθενής.

VIII

1.Ἀδιαλείπτως οὖν προσκαρτερῶμεν τῇ ἐλπίδι ἡμῶν καὶ τῷ ἀρραβῶνι τῆς δικαιοσύνης ἡμῶν, ὅς ἐστι Χριστὸς Ἰησοῦς, ὃς ἀνήγκεν ἡμῶν τὰς ἁμαρτίας τῷ ἰδίῳ σώματι ἐπὶ τὸ ξύλον, ὃς ἁμαρτίαν οὐκ ἐποίησεν, οὐδὲ εὑρέθη δόλος ἐν τῷ στόματι αὐτοῦ· ἀλλὰ δι' ἡμᾶς, ἵνα ζήσωμεν ἐν αὐτῷ, πάντα ὑπέμεινεν. 2. μιμηταὶ οὖν γενώμεθα τῆς ὑπομονῆς αὐτοῦ, καὶ ἐὰν πάσχωμεν διὰ τὸ ὄνομα αὐτοῦ, δοξάζωμεν αὐτόν. τοῦτον γὰρ ἡμῖν τὸν ὑπογραμμὸν ἔθηκε δι' ἑαυτοῦ, καὶ ἡμεῖς τοῦτο ἐπιστεύσαμεν.

IX

1.Παρακαλῶ οὖν πάντας ὑμᾶς, πειθαρχεῖν τῷ λόγῳ τῆς δικαιοσύνης καὶ ἀσκεῖν πᾶσαν ὑπομονήν, ἣν καὶ εἴδατε κατ' ὀφθαλμοὺς οὐ μόνον ἐν τοῖς μακαρίοις Ἰγνατίῳ καὶ Ζωσίμῳ καὶ Ῥούφῳ, ἀλλὰ καὶ ἐν ἄλλοις τοῖς ἐξ ὑμῶν καὶ ἐν αὐτῷ Παύλῳ καὶ τοῖς λοιποις ἀποστόλοις· 2. πεπεισμένους ὅτι οὗτοι πάντες οὐκ εἰς κενὸν ἔδραμον, ἀλλ' ἐν πίστει καὶ δικαιοσύνῃ, καὶ ὅτι εἰς τὸν ὀφειλόμενον αὐτοῖς τόπον εἰσὶ παρὰ τῷ κυρίῳ, ᾧ καὶ συνέπαθον. οὐ γὰρ τὸν νῦν ἠγάπησαν αἰῶνα, ἀλλὰ τὸν ὑπέρ ἡμῶν ἀποθανόντα καὶ δι' ἡμᾶς ὑπὸ τοῦ θεοῦ ἀναστάντα.

X

1.In his ergo state et domini exemplar sequimini, firmi in fide et immutabiles, fraternitatis amatores, diligentes invicem, in veritate sociati, mansuetudine domini alterutri praestolantes, nullum despicientes. 2. Cum possitis benefacere, nolite differre, quia eleëmosyna de morte liberat. Omnes vobis invicem subiecti estote, conversationem vestram irreprensibilem habentes in gentibus, ut ex bonis operibus vestris et vos laudem accipiatis et dominus in vobis non blasphemetur. 3. Vae autem per quem nomen domini blasphematur. Sobrietatem ergo docete omnes in qua et vos conversamini.

Polycarp to the Philippians

XI

1.Nimis contristatus sum pro Valente, qui presbyter factus est aliquando apud vos, quod sic ignoret is locum qui datus est ei. Moneo itaque ut abstinete vos ab omni malo. 2. Qui autem non potest se in his gubernare, quomodo alii pronuntiat hoc? Si quis non se abstinuerit ab avaritia, ab idolotatria conquinabitur et tamquam inter gentes iudicabitur, qui ignorant iudicium domini. Aut nescimus, quia sancti mundum iudicabunt? sicut Paulus docet. 3. Ego autem nihil tale sensi in vobis vel audivi, in quibus laboravit beatus Paulus, qui estis in principio episulae eius. De vobis etenim gloriatur in omnibus ecclesiis, quae dominum solae tunc cognoverant; nos autem nondum cognoveramus. 4. Valde ergo, fratres, constristor pro illo et pro coniuge eius, quibus det dominus paenitentiam veram. Sobrii ergo estote et vos in hoc; et non sicut inimicos tales existimetis, sed sicut passibilia membra et errantia eos revocate, ut omnium vestrum corpus salvetis. Hoc enim agentes vos ipsos aedificatis.

XII

1.Confido enim vos bene exercitatos esse in sacris literis et nihil vos latet; mihi autem non est concessum. Modo, ut his scripturis dictum est, irascimini et nolite peccare, et sol non occidat super iracundiam vestram. Beatus, qui meminerit; quod ego credo esse in vobis. 2. Deus autem et pater domini nostri Iesu Christi, et ipse sempiternus pontifex, dei filius Iesus Christus, aedificet vos in fide et veritate et in omni mansuetudine et sine iracundia et in patientia et in longanimitate et tolerantia et castitate; et det vobis sortem et partem inter sanctos suos et nobis vobiscum et omnibus, qui sunt sub caelo, qui credituri sunt in dominum nostrum et deum Iesum Christum et in ipsius patrem, qui resuscitavit eum a mortuis.

3.Pro omnibus sanctis orate. Orate etiam pro regibus et potestatibus et principibus atque pro persequentibus et odientibus vos et pro inimicis crucis, ut fructus vester manifestus sit in omnibus, ut sitis in illo perfecti.

XIII

1.Ἐγράψατέ μοι καὶ ὑμεῖς καὶ Ἰγνάτιος, ἵν', ἐάν τις ἀπέρχηται εἰς Σρίαν, καὶ τὰ παρ' ὑμῶν ἀποκομίσῃ γράμματα· ὅπερ ποιήσω, ἐὰν λάβω καιρὸν εὔθετον, εἴτε ἐγώ, εἴτε ὃν πέμπω πρεσβεύσοντα καὶ περὶ ὑμῶν. 2. τὰς ἐπιστολὰς Ἰγνατίου τὰς περμφθείσας ἡμῖν ὑπ' αὐτοῦ καὶ ἄλλας, ὅσας εἴχομεν παρ' ἡμῖν, ἐπέμψαμεν ὑμῖν, καθὼς ἐνετείλασθε· αἵτινες ὑποτεταγμέναι εἰσὶν τῇ ἐπιστολῇ ταύτῃ, ἐξ ὧν μεγάλα ὠφεληθῆναι δυνήσεσθε. περιέχουσιν γὰρ πίστιν καὶ ὑπομονὴν καὶ πᾶσαν οἰκοδομὴν τὴν εἰς τὸν κύριον ἡμῶν ἀνήκουσαν. *Et de ipso Ignatio et de his, qui cum eo sunt, quod certius agnoveritis significate.*

XIV

Haec vobis scripsi per Crescentem, quem in praesenti commendavi vobis et nunc commendo. Conversatus est enim nobiscum inculpabiliter; credo quia et vobiscum similiter. Sororem autem eius habebitis commendatam, eum venerit ad vos. Incolumes estote in domino Iesu Christo in gratia eum omnibus vestris. Amen.

Polycarp to the Philippians

Various English Translations:

THE EPISTLE OF POLYCARP

Translation by J.B. Lightfoot

Polycarp prologue:1

Polycarp and the presbyters that are with him unto the Church of God which sojourneth at Philippi; mercy unto you and peace from God Almighty and Jesus Christ our Savior be multiplied.

Polycarp 1:1

I rejoiced with you greatly in our Lord Jesus Christ, for that ye received the followers of the true Love and escorted them on their way, as befitted you--those men encircled in saintly bonds which are the diadems of them that be truly chosen of God and our Lord;

Polycarp 1:2

and that the steadfast root of your faith which was famed from primitive times abideth until now and beareth fruit unto our Lord Jesus Christ, who endured to face even death for our sins, *whom God raised, having loosed the pangs of Hades; on whom,*

Polycarp 1:3

though ye saw Him not, ye believe with joy unutterable and full of glory; unto which joy many desire to enter in; forasmuch as ye know that it is *by grace ye are saved, not of works*, but by the will of God through Jesus Christ.

Polycarp 2:1

Wherefore gird up your loins and serve God in fear and truth, forsaking the vain and empty talking and the error of the many, *for that ye have believed on Him that raised our Lord Jesus Christ from the dead and gave unto him glory* and a throne on His right hand; unto whom all things were made subject that are in heaven and that are on the earth; to whom every creature that hath breath doeth service; who cometh as *judge of quick and dead*; whose blood God will require of them that are disobedient unto Him.

Polycarp 2:2

Now *He that raised Him* from the dead *will raise us also*; if we do His will and walk in His commandments and love the things which He loved, abstaining from all unrighteousness, covetousness, love of money, evil speaking, false witness; *not rendering evil for evil or railing for railing* or blow for blow or cursing for cursing;

Polycarp 2:3

but remembering the words which the Lord spake, as He taught; *Judge not that ye be not judged. Forgive, and it shall be forgiven to you. Have mercy that ye may receive mercy. With what measure ye mete, it shall be measured to you again;* and again *Blessed are the poor and they that are persecuted for righteousness' sake, for theirs is the kingdom of God.*

Polycarp 3:1

These things, brethren, I write unto you concerning righteousness, not because I laid this charge upon myself, but because ye invited me.

Polycarp 3:2

For neither am I, nor is any other like unto me, able to follow the wisdom of the blessed and glorious Paul, who when he came among you taught face to face with the men of that day the word which concerneth truth carefully and surely; who also, when he was absent, wrote a letter unto you, into the which if ye look diligently, ye shall be able to be builded up unto the faith given to you,

Polycarp 3:3

which is the mother of us all, while hope followeth after and love goeth before--love toward God and Christ and toward our neighbor. For if any man be occupied with these, he hath fulfilled the commandment of righteousness; for he that hath love is far from all sin.

Polycarp 4:1

But the love of money is the beginning of all troubles. Knowing therefore that *we brought nothing into the world neither can we carry anything out*, let us arm ourselves with the armor of righteousness, and let us teach ourselves first to walk in the commandment of the Lord;

Polycarp 4:2

and then our wives also, to walk in the faith that hath been given unto them and in love and purity, cherishing their own husbands in all truth and loving all men equally in all chastity, and to train their children in the training of the fear of God.

Polycarp 4:3

Our widows must be sober-minded as touching the faith of the Lord, making intercession without ceasing for all men, abstaining from all calumny, evil speaking, false witness, love of money, and every evil thing, knowing that they are God's altar, and that all sacrifices are carefully inspected, and nothing escapeth Him either of their thoughts or intents or any of the secret things of the heart.

Polycarp 5:1

Knowing then that *God is not mocked*, we ought to walk worthily of His commandment and His glory.

Polycarp 5:2

In like manner deacons should be blameless in the presence of His righteousness, as deacons of God and Christ and not of men; not calumniators, not double-tongued, not lovers of money, temperate in all things, compassionate, diligent, walking according to the truth of the Lord who became a *minister (deacon) of all*. For if we be well pleasing unto Him in this present world, we shall receive the future world also, according as He promised us to raise us from the dead, and that if we conduct ourselves worthily of Him *we shall also reign with Him,* if indeed we have faith.

Polycarp 5:3

In like manner also the younger men must be blameless in all things, caring for purity before everything and curbing themselves from every evil. For it is a good thing to refrain from lusts in the world, for every *lust warreth against the Spirit*, and *neither whoremongers nor effeminate persons nor defilers of themselves with men shall*

Polycarp to the Philippians

inherit the kingdom of God, neither they that do untoward things. Wherefore it is right to abstain from all these things, submitting yourselves to the presbyters and deacons as to God and Christ.

The virgins must walk in a blameless and pure conscience.

Polycarp 6:1

And the presbyters also must be compassionate, merciful towards all men, *turning back the sheep that are gone astray, visiting all the infirm, not neglecting a widow or an orphan or a poor man: but providing always for that which is honorable in the sight of God and of men*, abstaining from all anger, respect of persons, unrighteous judgment, being far from all love of money, not quick to believe anything against any man, not hasty in judgment, knowing that we all are debtors of sin.

Polycarp 6:2

If then we entreat the Lord that He would forgive us, we also ought to forgive: for we are before the eyes of our Lord and God, and we must *all stand at the judgment-seat of Christ*, and *each man must give an account of himself.*

Polycarp 6:3

Let us therefore so serve Him with fear and all reverence, as He himself gave commandment and the Apostles who preached the Gospel to us and the prophets who proclaimed beforehand the coming of our Lord; being zealous as touching that which is good, abstaining from offenses and from the false brethren and from them that bear the name of the Lord in hypocrisy, who lead foolish men astray.

Polycarp 7:1

For every one *who shall not confess that Jesus Christ is come in the flesh, is antichrist*: and whosoever shall not confess the testimony of the Cross, is of the devil; and whosoever shall pervert the oracles of the Lord to his own lusts and say that there is neither resurrection nor judgment, that man is the firstborn of Satan.

Polycarp 7:2

Wherefore let us forsake the vain doing of the many and their false teachings, and turn unto the word which was delivered unto us from the beginning, *being sober unto prayer* and constant in fastings, entreating the all-seeing God with supplications that *He bring us not into temptation*, according as the Lord said, *The Spirit is indeed willing, but the flesh is weak.*

Polycarp 8:1

Let us therefore without ceasing hold fast by our hope and by the earnest of our righteousness, which is Jesus Christ who *took up our sins in His own body upon the tree, who did no sin, neither was guile found in His mouth*, but for our sakes He endured all things, that we might live in Him.

Polycarp 8:2

Let us therefore become imitators of His endurance; and if we should suffer for His name's sake, let us glorify Him. For He gave this example to us in His own person, and we believed this.

Polycarp 9:1

I exhort you all therefore to be obedient unto the word of righteousness and to practice all endurance, which also ye saw with your own eyes in the blessed

Ignatius and Zosimus and Rufus, yea and in others also who came from among yourselves, as well as in Paul himself and the rest of the Apostles;

Polycarp 9:2

being persuaded that all these *ran not in vain* but in faith and righteousness, and that they are in their due place in the presence of the Lord, with whom also they suffered. For they *loved not the present world*, but Him that died for our sakes and was raised by God for us.

Polycarp 10:1

Stand fast therefore in these things and follow the example of the Lord, *being firm in the faith* and *immovable, in love of the brotherhood kindly affectioned one to another*, partners with the truth, *forestalling one another* in the gentleness of the Lord, despising no man.

Polycarp 10:2

When ye are able to do good, defer it not, for *Pitifulness delivereth from death. Be ye all subject one to another, having your conversation* unblamable *among the gentiles, that your good works* both ye may receive praise and the Lord may not be blasphemed in you.

Polycarp 10:3

But *woe to him through whom the name of the Lord be blasphemed*. Therefore teach all men soberness, in which ye yourselves also walk.

Polycarp 11:1

I was exceedingly grieved for Valens, who aforetime was a presbyter among you, because he is so ignorant of the office which was given unto him. I warn you therefore that ye refrain from covetousness, and that ye be pure and truthful. Refrain from all evil.

Polycarp 11:2

But he who cannot govern himself in these things, how doth he enjoin this upon another? If a man refrain not from covetousness, he shall be defiled by idolatry, and shall be judged as one of the Gentiles who *know not the judgment of the Lord, Nay, know we not, that the saints shall judge the world*, as Paul teacheth?

Polycarp 11:3

But I have not found any such thing in you, neither have heard thereof, among whom the blessed Paul labored, who were his *letters* in the beginning. For *he boasteth of you in* all those *churches* which alone at that time knew God; for we knew Him not as yet.

Polycarp 11:4

Therefore I am exceedingly grieved for him and for his wife, unto whom may the Lord grant true repentance. Be ye therefore yourselves also sober herein, and *hold not such as enemies* but restore them as frail and erring members, that ye may save the whole body of you. For so doing, ye do edify one another.

Polycarp 12:1

Polycarp to the Philippians

For I am persuaded that ye are well trained in the sacred writings, and nothing is hidden from you. But to myself this is not granted. Only, as it is said in these scriptures, *Be ye angry and sin not*, and *Let not the sun set on your wrath*. Blessed is he that remembereth this; and I trust that this is in you.

Polycarp 12:2

Now may the God and Father of our Lord Jesus Christ, and the eternal High-priest Himself the [Son of God Jesus Christ, build you up in faith and truth, and in all gentleness and in all avoidance of wrath and in forbearance and long suffering and in patient endurance and in purity; and may He grant unto you a lot and portion among His saints, and to us with you, and to all that are under heaven, who shall believe on our Lord and God Jesus Christ and on His Father *that raised him from the dead.*

Polycarp 12:3

Pray for all the saints. Pray also *for kings* and powers and princes and *for them that persecute* and hate *you* and for *the enemies of the cross*, that your fruit may be *manifest among all men*, that ye may be perfect in Him.

Polycarp 13:1

Ye wrote to me, both ye yourselves and Ignatius, asking that if any one should go to Syria he might carry thither the letters from you. And this I will do, if I get a fit opportunity, either I myself, or he whom I shall send to be ambassador on your behalf also.

Polycarp 13:2

The letters of Ignatius which were sent to us by him, and others as many as we had by us, we send unto you, according as ye gave charge; the which are subjoined to this letter; from which ye will be able to gain great advantage. For they comprise faith and endurance and every kind of edification, which pertaineth unto our Lord. Moreover concerning Ignatius himself and those that were with him, if ye have any sure tidings, certify us.

Polycarp 14:1

I write these things to you by Crescens, whom I commended to you recently and now commend unto you: for he hath walked blamelessly with us; and I believe also with you in like manner. But ye shall have his sister commended, when she shall come to you. Fare ye well in the Lord Jesus Christ in grace, ye and all yours. Amen.

POLYCARP
TO THE PHILIPPIANS

CHAPTER 0

Greeting

1 Polycarp and the Elders with him to the Church of God sojourning in Philippi; mercy and peace from God Almighty and Jesus Christ our Saviour be multiplied to you.

CHAPTER 1

The hospitality of the Philippians -- Their faith

1 I rejoice greatly with you in our Lord Jesus Christ that you
have followed the pattern of true love, and have helped on their
way, as opportunity was given you, those who were bound in
chains, which become the saints, and are the diadems of those
who have been truly chosen by God and our Lord. 2 I rejoice
also that your firmly rooted faith, which was famous in past
years, still flourishes and bears fruit unto our Lord Jesus Christ,
who endured for our sins, even to the suffering of death, "whom
God raised up, having loosed the pangs of Hades, 3 in whom,
though you did not see him, you believed in unspeakable and
glorified joy," -- into which joy many desire to come, knowing
that "by grace ye are saved, not by works" but by the will of
God through Jesus Christ.

CHAPTER 2

Exhortation to virtue -- The hope of resurrection -- The Lord's Teaching

1 "Wherefore girding up your loins serve God in fear" and truth, putting aside empty vanity and vulgar error, "believing on him who raised up our Lord Jesus Christ from the dead and gave him glory," and a throne on his right hand, "to whom are subject all things in heaven and earth," whom all breath serves, who is coming as "the Judge of the living and of the dead," whose blood God will require from them who disobey him.
2 Now "he who raised him" from the dead "will also raise us up" if we do his will, and walk in his commandments and love the things which he loved, refraining from all unrighteousness, covetousness, love of money, evil speaking, false witness, "rendering not evil for evil, or railing for railing," or blow for blow, or curse for curse, 3 but remembering what the Lord taught when he said, "Judge not that ye be not judged, forgive and it shall be forgiven unto you, be merciful that ye may obtain mercy, with what measure ye mete, it shall be measured to you again," and, "Blessed are the poor, and they who are persecuted for righteousness' sake, for theirs is the Kingdom of God."

Polycarp to the Philippians

CHAPTER 3

Polycarp's reason for writing: the invitation ofthe Philippians

1 These things, brethren, I write to you concerning righteousness, not at my own instance, but because you first invited me. 2 For neither am I, nor is any other like me, able to follow the wisdom of the blessed and glorious Paul, who when he was among you in the presence of the men of that time taught accurately and stedfastly the word of truth, and also when he was absent wrote letters to you, from the study of which you will be able to build yourselves up into the faith given you; 3 "which is the mother of us all" when faith follows, and love of God and Christ and neighbour goes before. For if one be in this company he has fulfilled the command of righteousness, for he who has love is far from all sin.

CHAPTER 4

Exhortations to virtue

1 "But the beginning of all evils is the love of money." Knowing
therefore that "we brought nothing into the world and we can
take nothing out of it," let us arm ourselves with the armour
of righteousness, and let us first of all teach ourselves to walk
in the commandment of the Lord; 2 next teach our wives to
remain in the faith given to them, and in love and purity, tenderly
loving their husbands in all truth, and loving all others equally
in all chastity, and to educate their children in the fear of God.
3 Let us teach the widows to be discreet in the faith of the Lord,
praying ceaselessly for all men, being far from all slander, evil
speaking, false witness, love of money, and all evil, knowing
that they are the altar of God, and that all offerings are tested,
and that nothing escapes him of reasonings or thoughts, or of
"the secret things of the heart."

CHAPTER 5

Christian obligations to a virtuous life

1 Knowing then that "God is not mocked," we ought to walk worthily of his commandment and glory. 2 Likewise must the deacons be blameless before his righteousness, as the servants of God and Christ and not of man, not slanderers, not double-tongued, not lovers of money, temperate in all things, compassionate, careful, walking according to the truth of the Lord, who was the "servant of all." For if we please him in this present world we shall receive from him that which is to come; even as he promised us to raise us from the dead, and that if we are worthy citizens of his community, "we shall also reign with him," if we have but faith. 3 Likewise also let the younger men be blameless in all things; caring above all for purity, and curbing themselves from all evil; for it is good to be cut off from the lust of the things in the world, because "every lust warreth against the Spirit, and neither fornicators nor the effeminate nor sodomites shall inherit the Kingdom of God," nor they who do iniquitous things. Wherefore it is necessary to refrain from all these things, and to be subject to the presbyters and deacons as to God and Christ. The virgins must walk with a blameless and pure conscience.

CHAPTER 6

The duties of the presbyters -- Forgiveness -- The service of God

1 And let the presbyters also be compassionate, merciful to all, bringing back those that have wandered, caring for all the weak, neglecting neither widow nor orphan nor poor, but "ever providing for that which is good before God and man," refraining from all wrath, respect of persons, unjust judgment, being far from all love of money, not quickly believing evil of any, not hasty in judgment, knowing that "we all owe the debt of sin." 2 If then we pray the Lord to forgive us, we also ought to forgive, for we stand before the eyes of the Lord and of God, and "we must all appear before the judgment seat of Christ, and each must give an account of himself." 3 So then "let us serve him with fear and all reverence," as he himself commanded us, and as did the Apostles, who brought us the Gospel, and the Prophets who foretold the coming of our Lord. Let us be zealous for good, refraining from offence, and from the false brethren, and from those who bear the name of the Lord in hypocrisy, who deceive empty-minded men.

The introductory formula "knowing that" renders it probable that these words are a quotation, but the source is unknown.

CHAPTER 7

Warning against heresy

1 "For everyone who does not confess that Jesus Christ has come in the flesh is an anti-Christ"; and whosoever does not confess the testimony of the Cross is of the devil: and whosoever perverts the oracles of the Lord for his own lusts, and says that there is neither resurrection nor judgment, -- this man is the first-born of Satan. 2 Wherefore, leaving the foolishness of the crowd, and their false teaching, let us turn back to the word which was delivered to us in the beginning, "watching unto prayer" and persevering in fasting, beseeching the all-seeing God in our supplications "to lead us not into temptation," even as the Lord said, "The spirit is willing, but the flesh is weak."

This phrase, according to Irenaeus (Adv. Haer. /:) was applied, presumably later, by Polycarp to Marcion.

CHAPTER 8

Perseverance

1 Let us then persevere unceasingly in our hope, and in the pledge of our righteousness, that is in Christ Jesus, "who bare our sins in his own body on the tree, who did no sin, neither was guile found in his mouth," but for our sakes, that we might live in him, he endured all things. 2 Let us then be imitators of his

endurance, and if we suffer for his name's sake let us glorify him. For this is the example which he gave us in himself, and this is what we have believed.

CHAPTER 9

The examples of the martyrs

1 Now I beseech you all to obey the word of righteousness, and
to endure with all the endurance which you also saw before your
eyes, not only in the blessed Ignatius, and Zosimus, and Rufus,
but also in others among yourselves, and in Paul himself, and
in the other Apostles; 2 being persuaded that all of these "ran
not in vain," but in faith and righteousness, and that they are
with the Lord in the "place which is their due," with whom they
also suffered. For they did not "love this present world" but him
who died on our behalf, and was raised by God for our sakes.

CHAPTER 10

Perseverance in philanthropy and good works

1 Stand fast therefore in these things and follow the example of the Lord, "firm and unchangeable in faith, loving the brotherhood, affectionate to one another," joined together in the truth, forestalling one another in the gentleness of the Lord, despising no man. 2 When you can do good defer it not, "for almsgiving sets free from death; be ye all subject one to the other, having your conversation blameless among the Gentiles," that you may receive praise "for your good works" and that the Lord be not blasphemed in you. 3 "But woe to him through whom the name of the Lord is blasphemed." Therefore teach sobriety to all and show it forth in your own lives.

CHAPTER 11

Valens -- Against avarice -- The treatment of Valens

1 I am deeply sorry for Valens, who was once made a presbyter among you, that he so little understands the place which was given to him. I advise, therefore, that you keep from avarice, and be pure and truthful. Keep yourselves from all evil. 2 For how may he who cannot attain self-control in these matters enjoin it on another? If any man does not abstain from avarice he will be defiled by idolatry, and shall be judged as if he were among the Gentiles who "know not the judgment of God." Or do we "not know that the saints shall judge the world?" as Paul teaches. 3 But I have neither perceived nor heard any such thing among you, among whom the blessed Paul laboured, who are praised in the beginning of his Epistle. For concerning you he boasts in all the Churches who then alone had known the Lord, for we had not yet known him. 4 Therefore, brethren, I am deeply sorry for him [i.e. Valens] and for his wife, and "may the Lord grant them true repentance." Therefore be yourselves also moderate in this matter, and "do not regard such men as enemies," but call them back as fallible and straying members, that you may make whole the body of you all. For in doing this you edify yourselves.

The Greek was perhaps 'tois ousin en arche epistolais autou', and ought to be rendered "who were his epistles in the beginning," with a reference to 2 Cor. 3:2.

CHAPTER 12

The need of forgiveness -- Prayer for blessing

1 For I am confident that you are well versed in the Scriptures, and from you nothing is hid; but to me this is not granted. Only, as it is said in these Scriptures, "Be ye angry and sin not," and "Let not the sun go down upon your wrath." Blessed is the man who remembers this, and I believe that it is so with you.
2 Now may God and the Father of our Lord Jesus Christ, and the "eternal Priest" himself, Jesus Christ, the Son of God, build you up in faith and truth, and in all gentleness, and without wrath, and in patience, and in longsuffering, and endurance, and purity, and may he give you lot and part with his saints, and to us with you, and to all under heaven who shall believe in our Lord and God Jesus Christ and in his "Father who raised him from the dead." 3 "Pray for all the saints. Pray also for the Emperors," and for potentates, and princes, and for "those who persecute you and hate you," and for "the enemies of the Cross" that "your fruit may be manifest among all men, that you may be perfected" in him.

---

1. *Probably this ought to be regarded as a quotation from the letter of the Philippians to Polycarp.*

2. *"Pro regibus' is no doubt a translation of 'huper basileon' and 'basileus' is regularly used as the title of the Emperor.*

CHAPTER 13

Ignatius and the Church in Syria

1 Both you and Ignatius wrote to me that if anyone was going to Syria he should also take your letters. I will do this if I have a convenient opportunity, either myself or the man whom I am sending as a representative for you and me. 2 We send you, as you asked, the letters of Ignatius, which were sent to us by him, and others which we had by us. These are subjoined to this letter, and you will be able to benefit greatly from them. For they contain faith, patience, and all the edification which pertains to our Lord. Let us know anything further which you have heard about Ignatius himself and those who are with him.

CHAPTER 14

Final greetings

1 I have written this to you by Crescens, whom I commended to you when I was present, and now commend again. For he has behaved blamelessly among us, and I believe that he will do the same with you. His sister shall be commended to you

Polycarp to the Philippians

when she comes to you. Farewell in the Lord Jesus Christ in grace, with all who are yours. Amen.